Ll

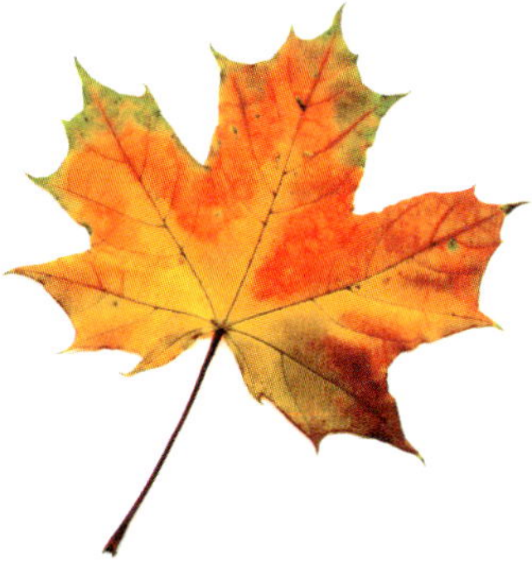

Ransom

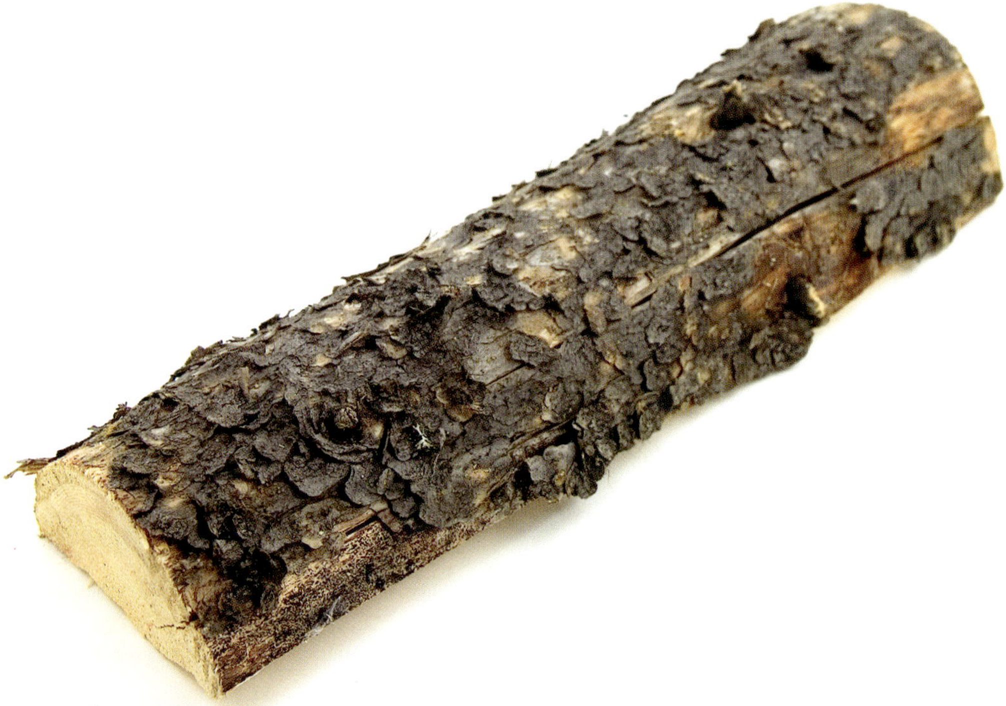

log

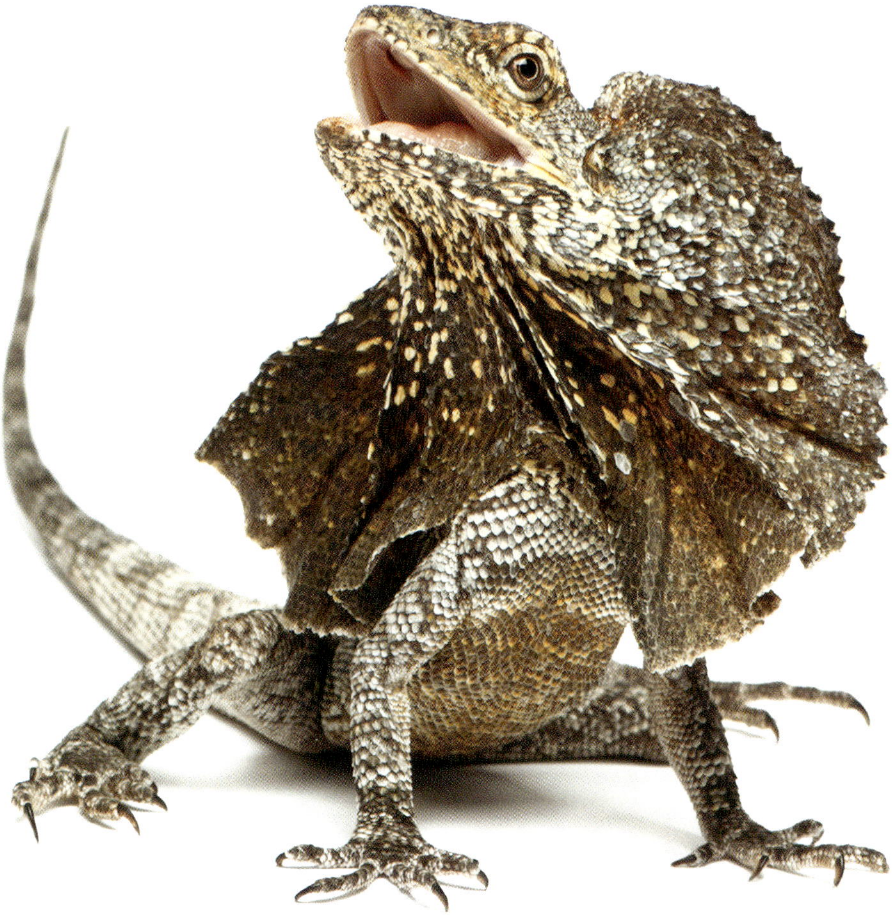

lizard

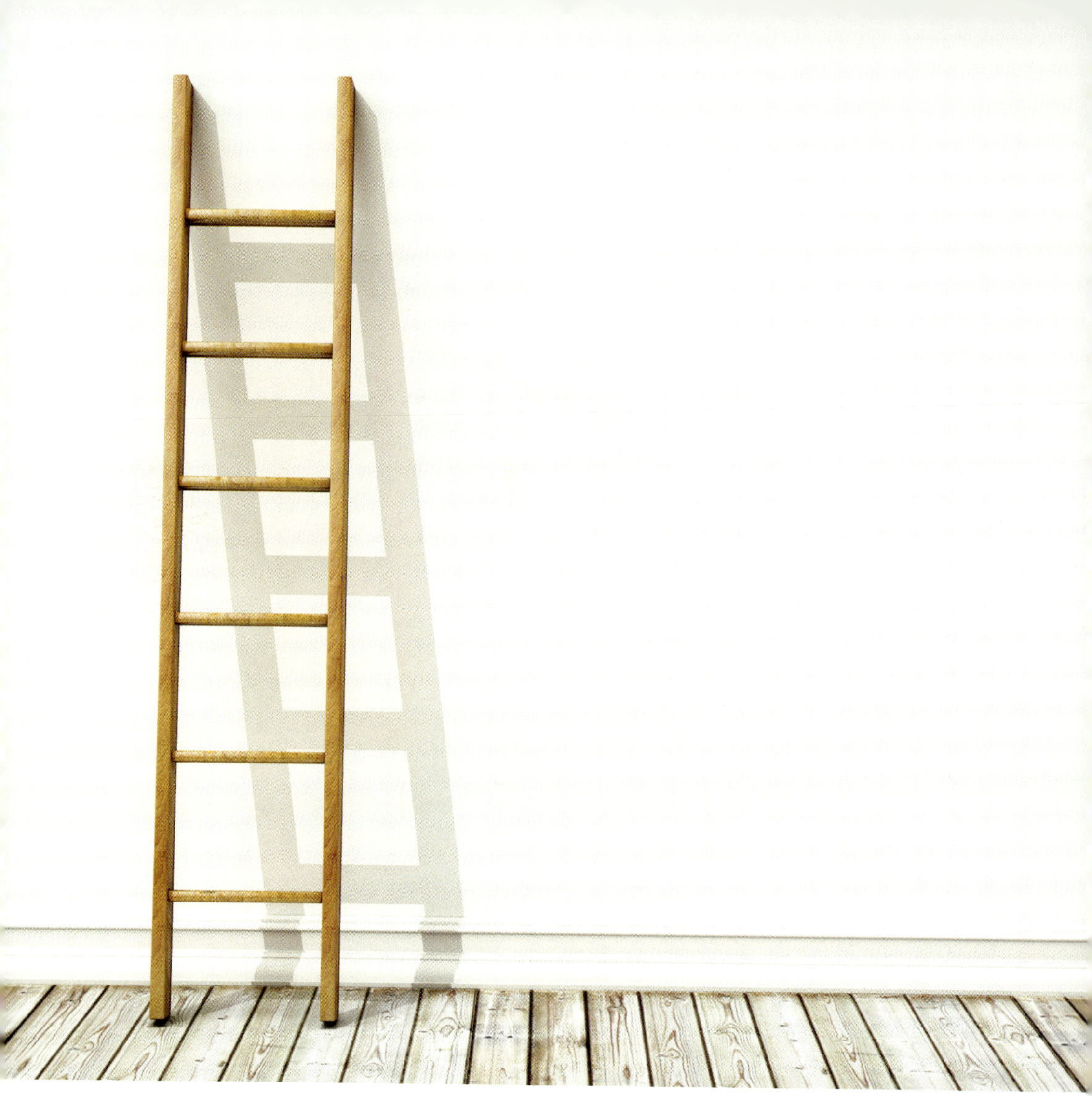

ladder

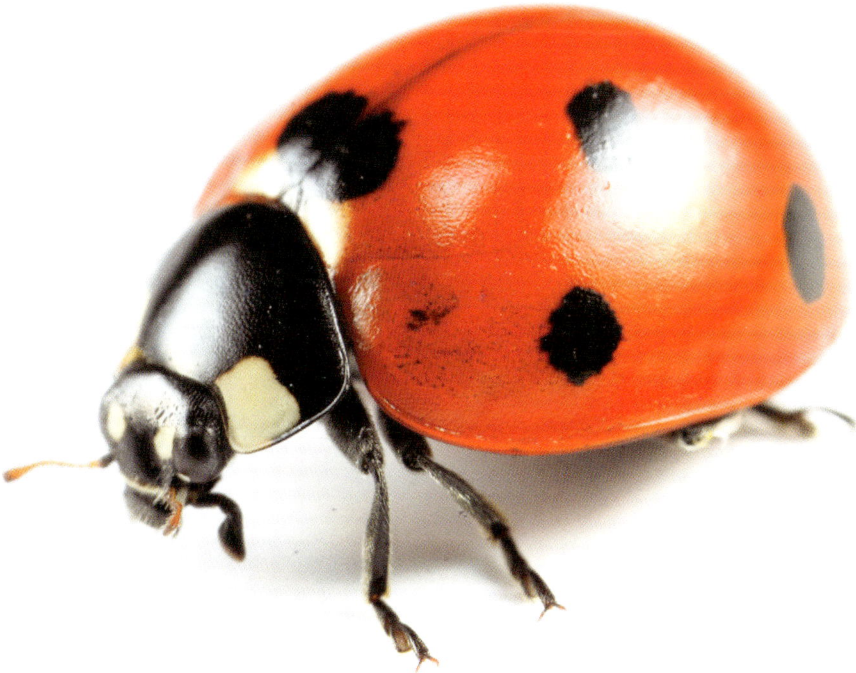

ladybird

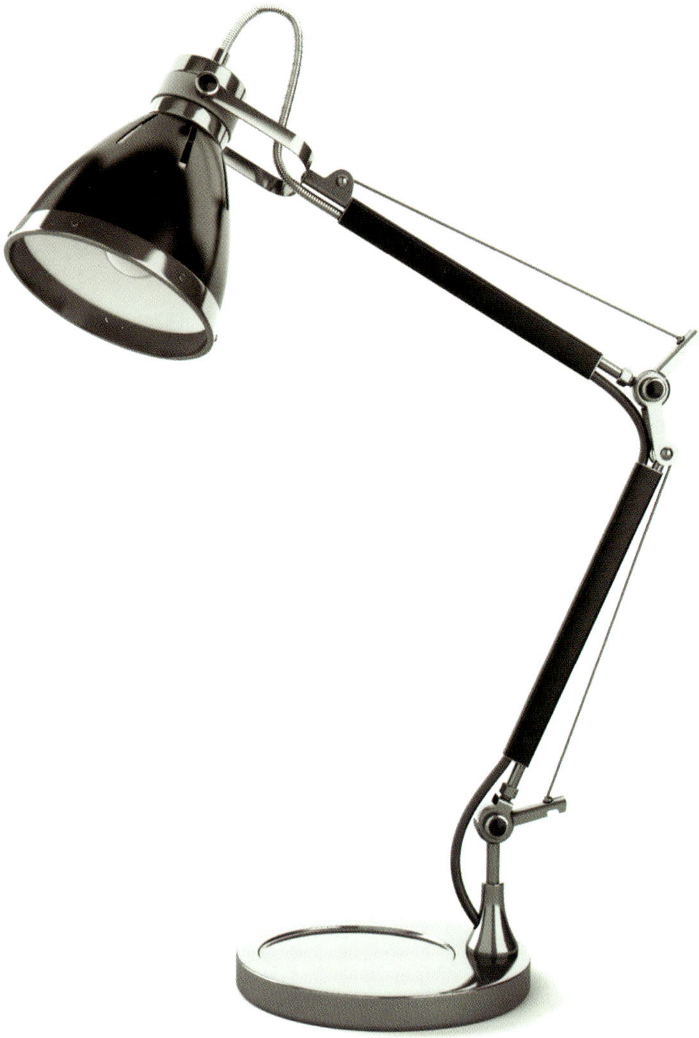

lamp

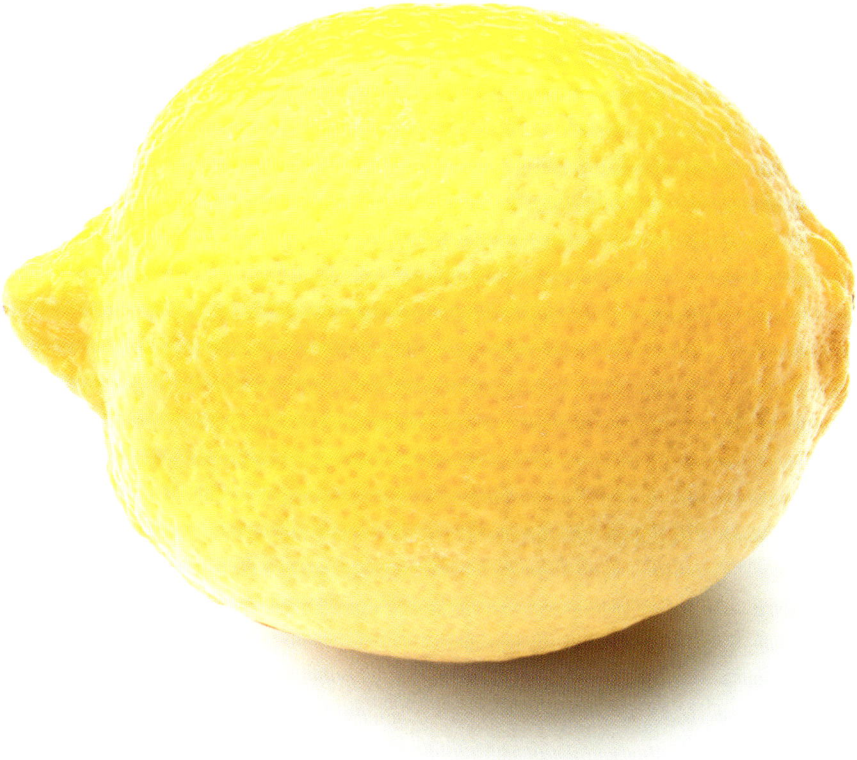

lemon

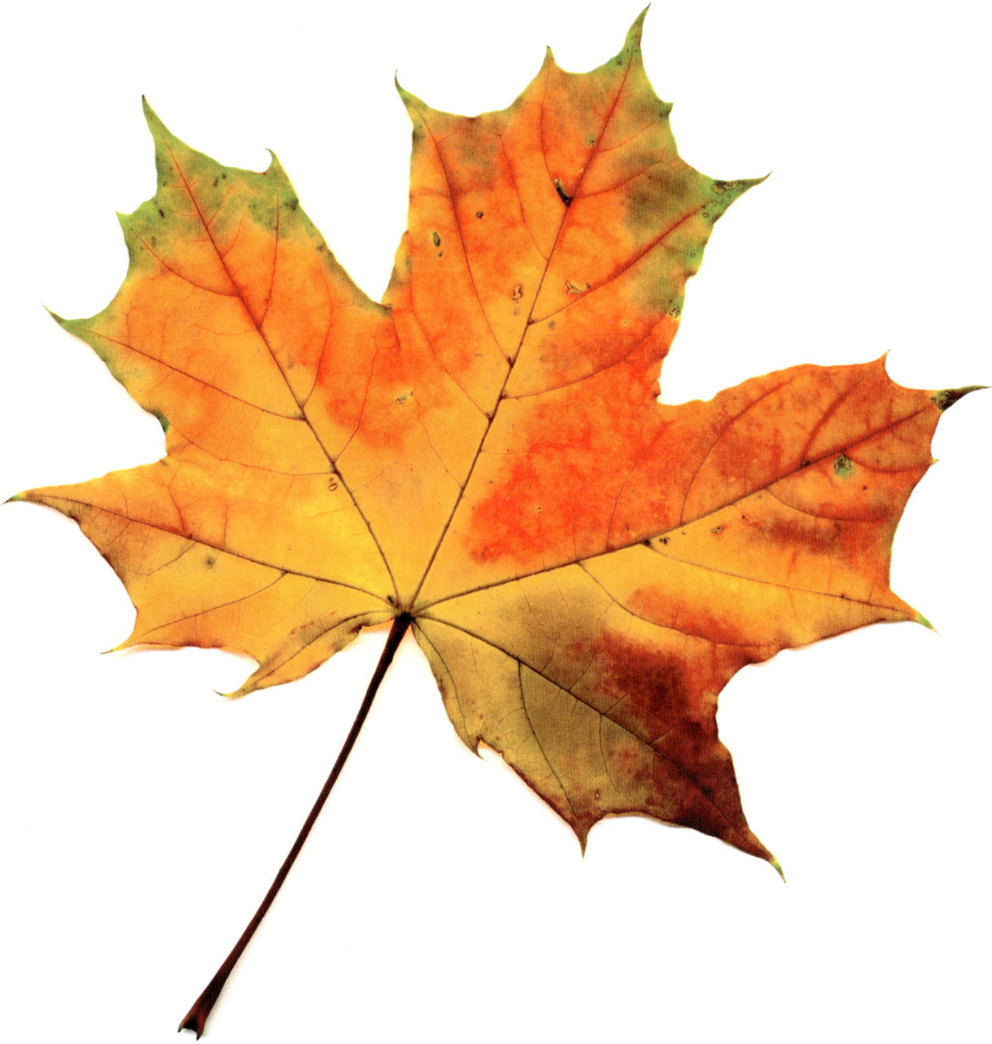

leaf

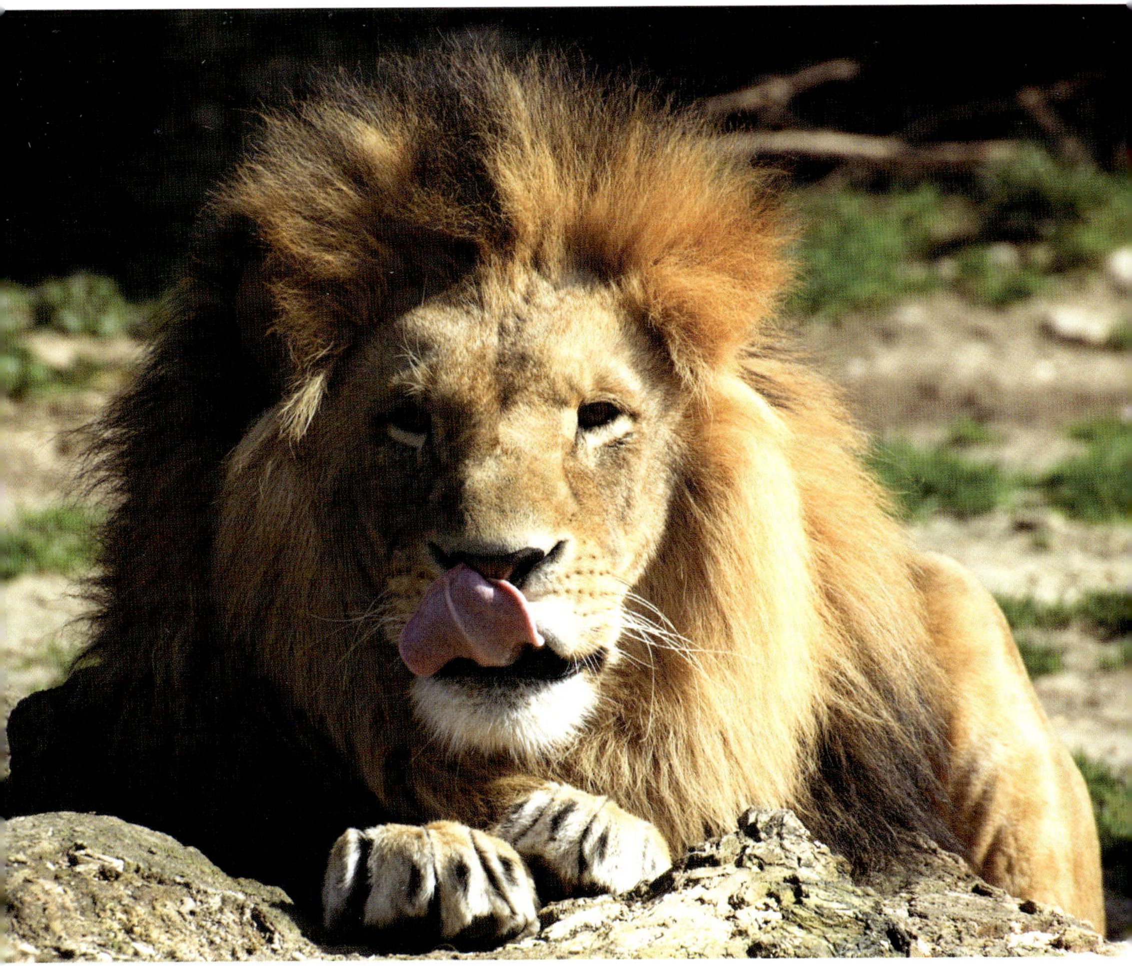

lion

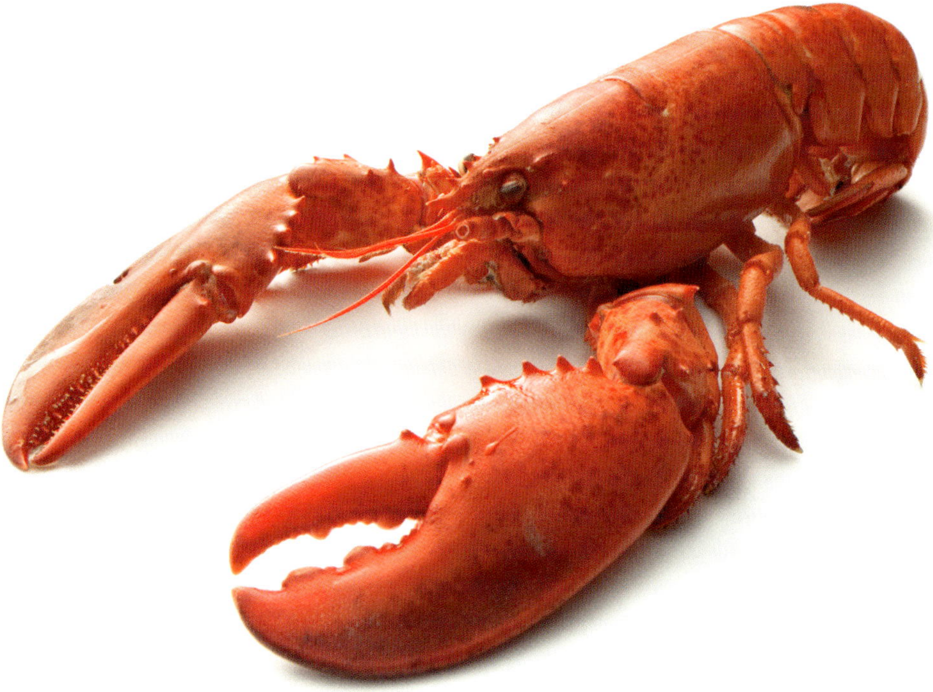

Ll

log

lizard

ladder

ladybird

lamp

lemon

leaf

lion